# NEVER *touch* a shark!

## STICKER ACTIVITY BOOK

Enter a sea-riously cool world in this activity book!

Search for the hidden sharks, ride the waves, and sticker a rock band.

Where there is a missing sticker, you will see an empty shape. Search the sticker pages to find the missing sticker.

Don't forget to press out games, a jaw-some puzzle, shark glasses and much more from the card pages at the back of the book!

make believe ideas

# Volcano view

Search the scene for the things below.
Trace the check marks when you find them.

# Count along!

Use color and stickers to finish the page.
Then count to five!

**1**
one

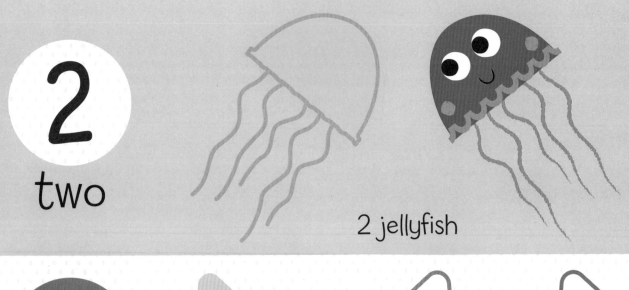

1 turtle

**2**
two

2 jellyfish

**3**
three

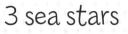

3 sea stars

**4** four

4 seahorses

**5** five

5 sharks

5

# Sports day!

Use color and stickers to finish the crowd.

How many yellow flags can you count? Write the answer.
..........

# Follow the lines to see who won the swimming trophy.

# Famous fish

Find five differences between the pictures.

# Check the boxes when you find them.

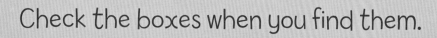

# Toy time

Count the toys under each animal.
Write the answers in the circles.

2

# Find me

Find and circle the shark that looks exactly like this.

# Seaweed tangle

Trace the path to guide the shark out of the seaweed.

Start here!

Finish

# Shark snacks

Draw a line to match each snack to the correct number.

**3**

three

**2**

two

**4**

four

# Treasure hunt

Find the stickers to finish the picture. Then color it.

How many crowns can you count? Write the answer.

.........

# Shark rock

Use color and stickers to finish the picture.

Draw a line to join the shells.

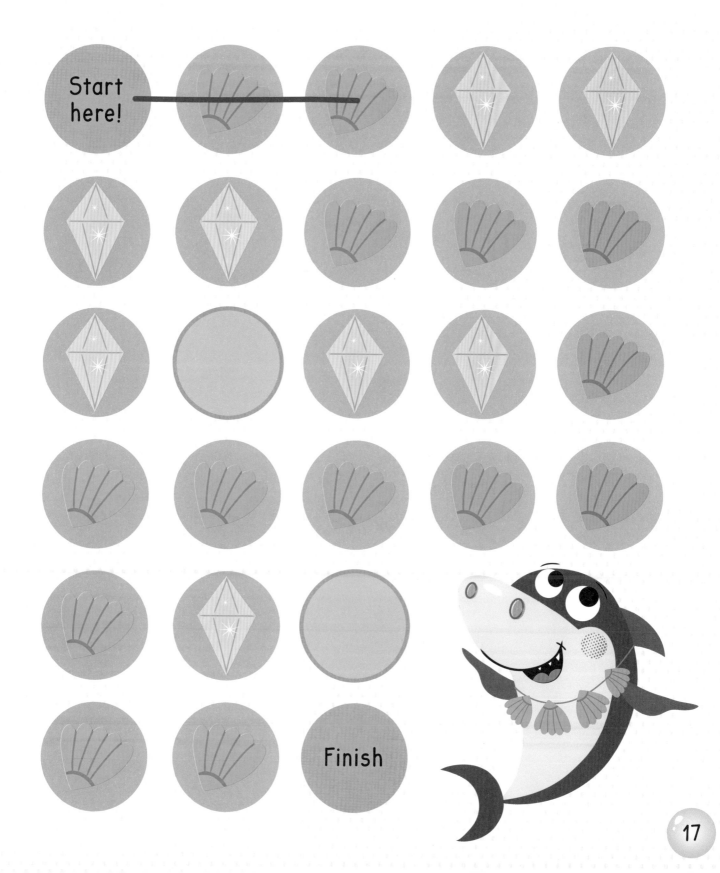

Start here!

Finish

# Playful patterns

Find the stickers to complete the patterns.

# Mini match

Draw lines to match the babies to their parents.

# Shark fun

Trace the words to find out what the sharks like to do for fun!

bake

read

race

sing

21

# Seahorse sprint

Color the seahorse. Use the dots to guide you.

# Swimming solo

Circle the one that doesn't belong in each row.

# Happy homes

Use color and stickers to finish the page.
Say the colors as you go!

purple

blue

green

orange

# Reef party

Search the picture for the creatures below.
Trace the check marks when you find them.

# Terrific teeth

Join the dots to finish the shark.
Then color the picture.

1

3

5

2

4

# Counting fish

Count the fish to finish the sums.

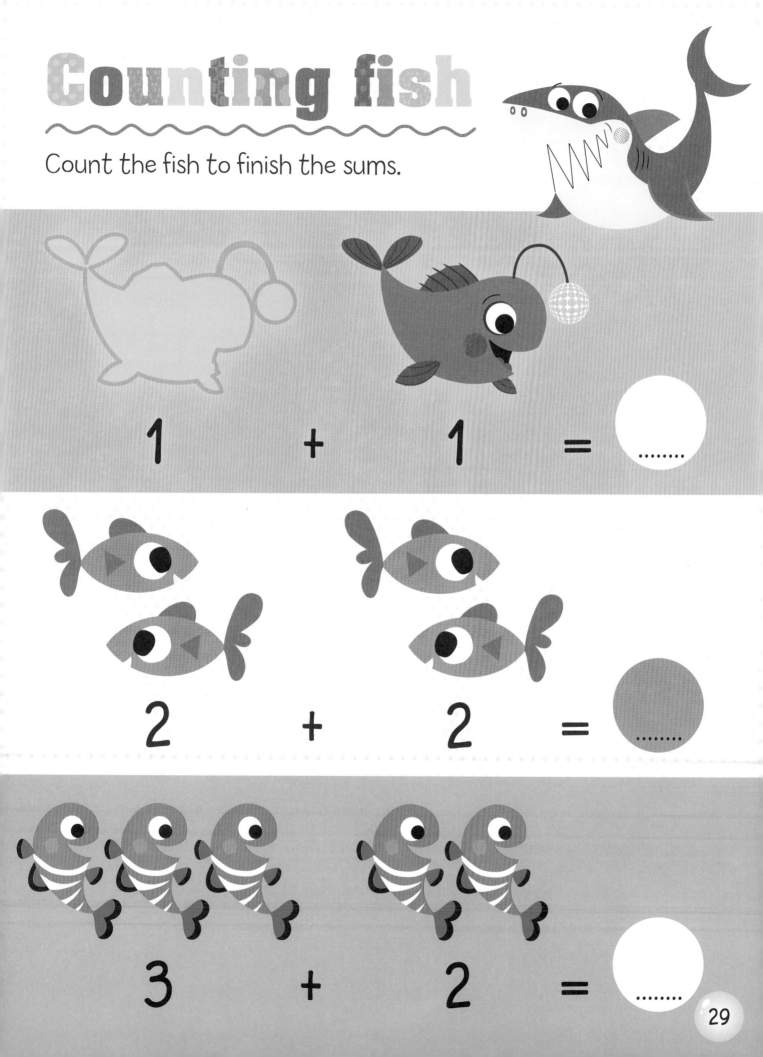

1 + 1 = ........

2 + 2 = ........

3 + 2 = ........

# Hide-and-seek

Circle five sharks hiding in the shipwreck.

# Wacky waves

Use a pencil to trace the trails.

# Talent show

Finish the picture with color and stickers.

# Letter links

Find and link the letters to spell the words.

crab    shark    fish

c — r    t    d    s    p

r    a    b    w    h

e    f    c    d    a    x

m    i    y    o    r

k    g    s    h    j    k

33

# Quick quiz

Find the missing stickers.
Then circle the fish to answer the questions below.

Who is the biggest?

Who is wearing sunglasses?

Who is purple and pink?

Who is the smallest?

# Copy me

Use color to make the pictures match.

36

# Friendly finds

Find your way through the maze to the puffer fish.
Use the key to guide you.

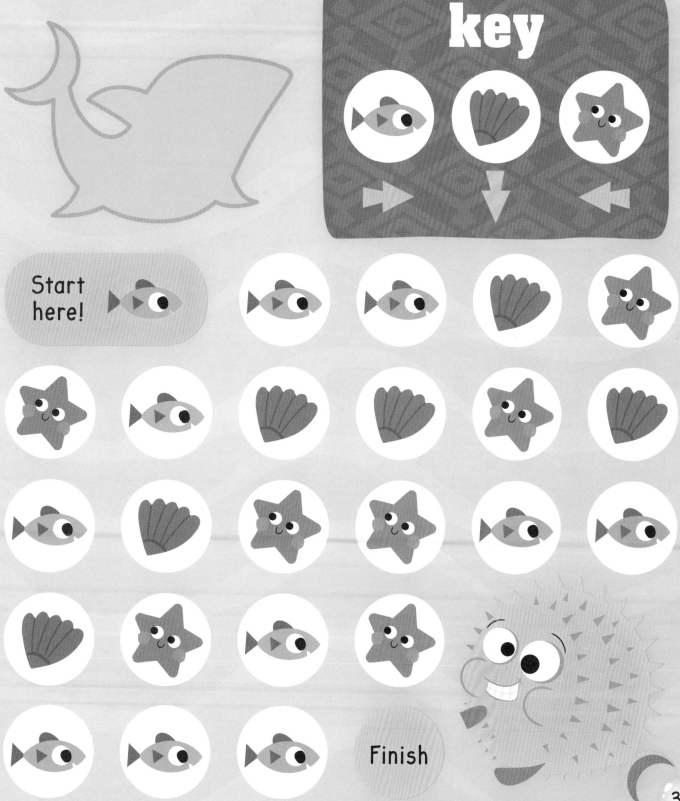

# Shark scribbles

Color the . . .

- sharks blue.
- turtles green.
- shells red.
- sea stars yellow.

Sticker the pink seahorses.

# Perfect partners

Draw lines to match the animals to their partners.
Who doesn't have a partner?

# Turtle trace

Trace the lines to finish the turtle.
Then color the picture.

# Shark skills

Follow the word **shark** to help the shark reach its home.

Start here!

Finish

42

# Sea search

Circle the fish that look like these.

# Shark snap

Use color to finish the picture.

# Shark glasses

1. Gently press out the frame, arms, and eye holes.
2. Slot the arms onto the frames.
3. Then put the glasses on!

1 Press out the cards and place them facedown on the table.

2 Turn over two cards at a time. If they match, put them to one side. If they don't, turn them over and try again.

3 Keep going until you've found all the pairs!

Pages 2-3

Pages 4-5

Pages 6-7

Pages 8-9

Pages 10-11

Pages 12-13

Pages 14-15

Page 16

Page 17

Pages 18-19

Pages 20-21

NEVER touch A dinoSaur!

Extra stickers

Page 22

Page 23

Pages 24-25

Pages 26-27

Page 28

Extra stickers

Page 29

Pages 30-31

Pages 32-33

Pages 34-35

Pages 36-37

Pages 38-39

Pages 40-41

Pages 42-43

Page 44

Extra stickers

Extra stickers